D0568816

THE FBI STORY

The FBI's Most Wanted

By Alan Wachtel

MASON CREST PUBLISHERS

Produced in association with Water Buffalo Books.
Design by Westgraphix LLC.

MASON CREST PUBLISHERS INC.
370 Reed Road
Broomall, Pennsylvania 19008
(866) MCP-BOOK (toll free)
www.masoncrest.com

Printed in the United States of America

First Printing

9 8 7 6 5 4 3 2 1

Library of Congress Cataloging-in-Publication Data

Wachtel, Alan, 1968-
        The FBI's most wanted / Alan Wachtel.
            p. cm. — (The FBI story)
        Includes bibliographical references and index.
        ISBN 978-1-4222-0562-4 (hardcover) — ISBN 978-1-4222-1376-6 (pbk.)
        1. United States. Federal Bureau of Investigation—Juvenile literature.
            2. Fugitives from justice—United States—Biography—Juvenile literature.
            3. Criminals—United States—Biography—Juvenile literature. I. Title.
HV8144.F43W33 2009
363.250973—dc22   2008047901

Publisher's note:
All quotations in this book come from original sources and contain the spelling and grammatical
inconsistencies of the original text.

CONTENTS

CHAPTER 1 Fugitives from the Law

On February 18, 1952, 24-year-old Arnold Schuster was riding the New York City subway. Something about the man standing near him looked familiar. When the man saw Schuster watching him, he looked down. Soon, Schuster realized that the man looked like Willie Sutton. Sutton was a famous bank robber—and one of the criminals on the Federal Bureau of Investigation (FBI) Ten Most Wanted **Fugitives** list. Schuster had seen Sutton's picture on a poster in his father's clothing store, where he worked. Knowing that Sutton liked to

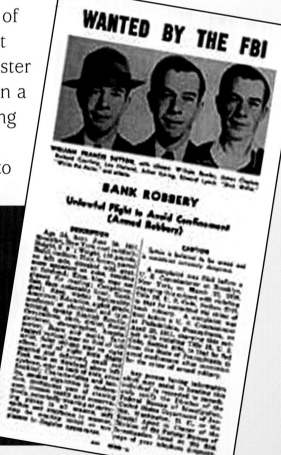

WANTED BY THE FBI

BANK ROBBERY
Unlawful Flight to Avoid Confinement
(Armed Robbery)

When clothing salesman Arnold Schuster saw Willie "The Actor" Sutton in a New York City subway, he recognized him as the criminal pictured on this Wanted poster. Sutton had a reputation as a dangerous, gun-toting bank robber with a flair for wearing disguises and expensive suits. His capture caused a sensation in the press and turned Schuster into an instant celebrity—and a marked man.

dress well, the FBI had distributed his picture to clothing stores. The FBI hoped that store workers would be on the lookout for the bank robber.

A Triumph for the FBI

The FBI's hopes were realized. As the events of the next few hours played out, it was clear that putting Willie Sutton on the Ten Most Wanted Fugitives list led directly to his arrest.

When the man got off the subway, Schuster followed him. The man walked to his car and found that it would not start. While the man was trying to start his car, Schuster tracked down two police officers and told them that he thought he had seen Willie Sutton. He said, "I know you're going to think I'm crazy . . . But I just saw Willie Sutton. He's right around the corner fixing a car."

The officers approached the man and checked his identification, which said his name was Charles Gordon. They let the man go. Back at the station, they told Detective Louis Weiner about how they thought they were about to catch Willie Sutton. Weiner wanted to question the man himself. The detective and the two officers brought the man back to the station to check his identification further. At first, the man acted innocent. Soon, however, he knew he was caught. The man admitted he was Willie Sutton and gave himself up.

Catching Sutton was a great victory for the police. They got one of the most **notorious** bank robbers in U.S. history off the streets. It was also a triumph for the FBI. By putting Sutton on the Ten Most Wanted Fugitives list, the FBI let people know what Sutton looked like and that he was on the loose. With this knowledge, ordinary citizens—such as Arnold

Schuster—have been able to play a crucial role in helping law enforcement agencies catch dangerous criminals. The spotting and arrest of Willie Sutton was a perfect example of how the Ten Most Wanted Fugitives list is intended to work.

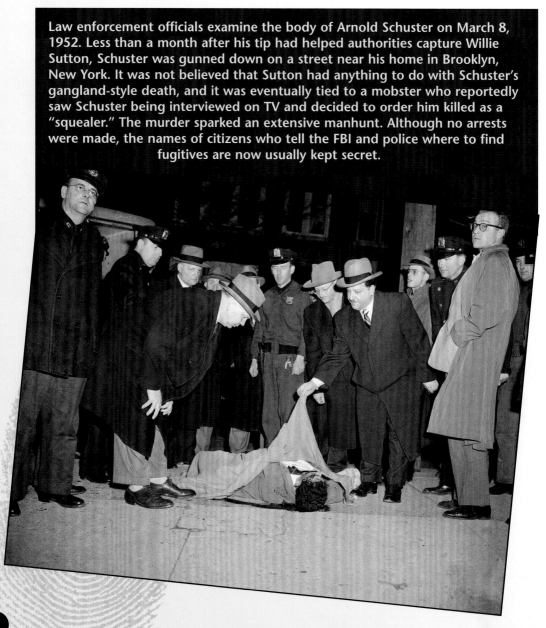

Law enforcement officials examine the body of Arnold Schuster on March 8, 1952. Less than a month after his tip had helped authorities capture Willie Sutton, Schuster was gunned down on a street near his home in Brooklyn, New York. It was not believed that Sutton had anything to do with Schuster's gangland-style death, and it was eventually tied to a mobster who reportedly saw Schuster being interviewed on TV and decided to order him killed as a "squealer." The murder sparked an extensive manhunt. Although no arrests were made, the names of citizens who tell the FBI and police where to find fugitives are now usually kept secret.

"Willie the Actor"

Willie Sutton was a hard criminal to catch, which is why the FBI needed Schuster's information. Sutton was also known as "Willie the Actor." The nickname came from a trick he used to commit bank robberies. In his **autobiography**, *I, Willie Sutton*, the criminal described an idea that occurred to him while he was thinking about a failed robbery:

> . . . I was walking along Broadway when I saw an armored truck stop in front of a business establishment after closing hours. Two of the uniformed guards approached the door, rang the bell, and were admitted. In a few moments they marched from the store, climbed into their truck and drove off. . . . I doubted very much if the clerk who admitted them to the store looked at their faces. He saw the uniforms and waved them in. The right uniform was an open sesame . . . that would unlock any door. That afternoon "Willie the Actor" was born.

Over and over, Sutton used disguises to help him get into the banks and other businesses that he robbed. He dressed up as a mailman, a **telegram** messenger, and a police officer. After being locked up in Philadelphia County Prison, in Homesburg, Pennsylvania, Sutton even dressed up as a prison guard in order to escape from jail.

Between the late 1920s and 1952, Willie Sutton commit-ted more than 100 robberies, stealing loot worth more than $2 million. The first two times he was caught, Sutton broke out of jail. With his long record of robberies and jailbreaks—

LONGEST AND SHORTEST TIME ON THE LIST

When the FBI lists a criminal on the Ten Most Wanted Fugitives list, officials have no idea how long it will take for the criminal to be caught. Billie Austin Bryant (right) had the shortest stay on the list—only two hours. Bryant was placed on the list on January 8, 1969. That day, he robbed a bank in Maryland and murdered two out of the three FBI agents who tracked him down after the robbery. Bryant fled the scene and hid in the attic of a nearby apartment building. When the man who lived in the apartment under the attic heard strange noises above him, he called the police. Bryant, it turned out, had accidentally trapped himself in the attic. With nowhere to run, he surrendered to the police.

As of 2009, Donald Eugene Webb has had the longest stay on the Ten Most Wanted Fugitives list. He was on the list from May 4, 1981, to March 31, 2007—almost 26 years. Webb was wanted for beating and murdering Gregory Patrick Adams, a Pennsylvania police chief, on December 4, 1980. Webb has not been seen since that day. In 2007, Webb was removed from the list to make room for other wanted fugitives. Authorities suspect that he may have died a long time ago. He is shown at right in photos from his Wanted poster—one taken in 1979 and the other an "age enhanced" image.

and his reputation for carrying a gun during robberies—Sutton earned a reputation as a dangerous criminal. He was the 11th fugitive ever to be added to the Ten Most Wanted list.

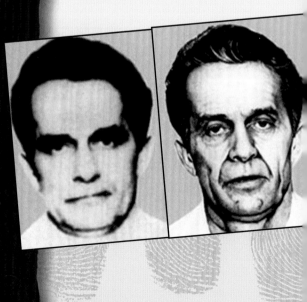

CHAPTER 2

Before the Ten Most Wanted List

The FBI did not establish the Ten Most Wanted Fugitives list until 1950. Long before then, though, the U.S. government was involved in catching criminals and enforcing the laws. Some crimes drew great attention in the media. The people who committed them were the most wanted criminals of their day, and they were portrayed as "wanted" in various ways even before the list became a part of the FBI's strategy for tracking them down.

"Identification Order Number 1," for William N. Bishop, an escaped military prisoner, became the Bureau's first Wanted poster when it appeared in 1919.

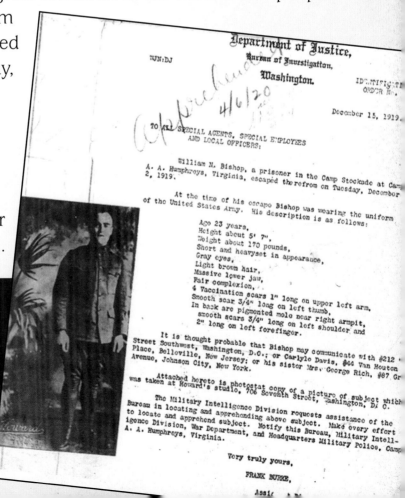

Department of Justice,
Bureau of Investigation,
Washington.

WJN:DJ

IDENTIFICATION
ORDER No.

December 15, 1919.

TO ALL SPECIAL AGENTS, SPECIAL EMPLOYEES AND LOCAL OFFICERS:

William N. Bishop, a prisoner in the Camp Stockade at Camp A. A. Humphreys, Virginia, escaped therefrom on Tuesday, December 2, 1919.

At the time of his escape Bishop was wearing the uniform of the United States Army. His description is as follows:

Age 23 years,
Height about 5' 7",
Weight about 170 pounds,
Short and heavyset in appearance,
Gray eyes,
Light brown hair,
Massive lower jaw,
Fair complexion,
4 Vaccination scars 1" long on upper left arm,
Smooth scar 3/4" long on left thumb,
In back are pigmented mole near right armpit,
smooth scars 3/4" long on left shoulder and
2" long on left forefinger.

It is thought probable that Bishop may communicate with #212 Street Southwest, Washington, D.C.; or Carlyle Davis, #44 Van Houten Place, Belleville, New Jersey; or his sister Mrs. George Rich, #87 Gr Avenue, Johnson City, New York.

Attached hereto is photostat copy of a picture of subject which was taken at Howard's studio, 706 Seventh Street, Washington, D. C.

The Military Intelligence Division requests assistance of the Bureau in locating and apprehending above subject. Make every effort to locate and apprehend said subject. Notify this Bureau, Military Intelligence Division, War Department, and Headquarters Military Police, Camp A. A. Humphreys, Virginia.

Very truly yours,

FRANK BURKE,

Assi...

The Early Days of Law Enforcement

In the early days of the United States, enforcement of laws was mainly the job of state governments. As trade grew between the states and transportation improved—allowing people to move easily from one state to another—leaders realized that the country needed a way to enforce laws across state lines. To meet this need, the U.S. government created the Department of Justice in 1870.

The Department of Justice, however, did not do its own investigating. The work of figuring out what happened in criminal cases was done by U.S. government lawyers, private detectives, or members of the **Secret Service.** By the end of the 19th century, Congress made it illegal for the government to use private detectives. Then, in the early 20th century, Congress cut the budget of the Treasury Department. The Treasury Department ran the Secret Service, and the budget cut made it impossible for the Justice Department to use agents from the Secret Service.

In 1908, Attorney General Charles Bonaparte—the head of the Justice Department—saw that the department needed its own agents. He hired a team of 34 agents, including 10 former Secret Service agents. This unit was the first agency of the federal government devoted to investigating crimes. At first, Bonaparte referred to the unit simply as "special agents." In 1909, the unit was named the Bureau of Investigation. It went through several names before it finally came to be known as the Federal Bureau of Investigation in 1935.

By 1935, the FBI had 568 agents and a yearly budget of more than $4.6 million. It also had a director—J. Edgar

J. Edgar Hoover ran the FBI from the time of his appointment as Director of the Bureau of Investigation in 1924 until his death in 1972. During that time the FBI grew into a respected national crime-fighting force. By the time of Hoover's death, *FBI* and *J. Edgar Hoover* had become household names, and each came under increasing public scrutiny as their powers and responsibilities grew.

Hoover—who was determined to build it into a well-organized and professional crime fighting force. Hoover was appointed Director of the Bureau in 1924 and ran it until his death in 1972. During the years that Hoover led the FBI, the number of agents grew to 8,659, and the budget topped $336 million. The FBI became a permanent part of American life.

Federal Law Enforcement Comes of Age

In the early 1930s, a number of well-known crimes shocked the nation. Many people spoke of a "crime wave," or a dramatic increase in the number of crimes. Newspapers wrote stories about crimes, and Hollywood made movies about crimes. It was during this time that the FBI became famous.

One of the most famous crimes of this era was the kidnapping of the Lindbergh baby. Charles Lindbergh was an aviator (pilot) who was famous for making a solo flight across the Atlantic Ocean in 1927. His wife, Anne Morrow Lindbergh, was a famous writer. On March 1, 1932, their baby son was kidnapped from their New Jersey home and held for **ransom**. The Lindberghs paid the ransom but still never saw their son

The kidnapping and subsequent murder of the son of Charles and Anne Morrow Lindbergh was one of several high-profile cases in which the FBI played a prominent role. This poster resembles the Wanted posters that the Bureau developed as part of its Ten Most Wanted Fugitives program in the 1950s.

WANTED

INFORMATION AS TO THE WHEREABOUTS OF

CHAS. A. LINDBERGH, JR.
OF HOPEWELL, N. J.

SON OF COL. CHAS. A. LINDBERGH
World-Famous Aviator

This child was kidnaped from his home in Hopewell, N. J., between 8 and 10 p. m. on Tuesday, March 1, 1932.

DESCRIPTION:

Age, 20 months   Hair, blond, curly
Weight, 27 to 30 lbs.   Eyes, dark blue
Height, 29 inches   Complexion, light
Deep dimple in center of chin
Dressed in one-piece coverall night suit

ADDRESS ALL COMMUNICATIONS TO
COL. H. N. SCHWARZKOPF, TRENTON, N. J., or
COL. CHAS. A. LINDBERGH, HOPEWELL, N. J.

ALL COMMUNICATIONS WILL BE TREATED IN CONFIDENCE

COL. H. NORMAN SCHWARZKOPF
Supt. New Jersey State Police, Trenton, N. J.

March 11, 1932

alive again. About two months after the kidnapping, the baby's body was found buried near Lindbergh's home.

President Franklin D. Roosevelt called in the FBI to take over the case. FBI agents distributed lists of the serial numbers of the bills used to pay the ransom. They worked to put together a **profile** of the murderer. Their efforts eventually led to the capture of a man named Bruno Hauptmann on September 19, 1934. At Hauptmann's trial, an FBI handwriting expert testified that Hauptmann had written the ransom notes left at the scene of the kidnapping. Hauptmann also had some of the ransom money. The Lindbergh baby case was one of the first famous criminal cases in which the FBI played a major role.

Public Enemies

A number of other famous cases helped the FBI make its name as a force in American crime fighting. Top government leaders such as President Franklin D. Roosevelt and Attorney General Homer S. Cummings promoted the idea that certain criminals were so dangerous to society that the federal government needed to expand its crime-fighting role. These criminals were known as "public enemies," and their crimes included bank robbery, kidnapping, and murder. The manhunts for public enemies made big news. They brought a great deal of attention to the role of the FBI in catching the most wanted criminals in the country.

Several of the public enemies became well known after the morning of June 17, 1933. On that day in Kansas City, Missouri, a group of law-enforcement officers—including four FBI agents—were moving a criminal, Frank Nash, to Leavenworth Penitentiary. All of a sudden, three gunmen ambushed them. The gunmen were the known criminals Vernon C. Miller, Adam Richetti, and Charles "Pretty Boy" Floyd. In the surprise attack, the gunmen killed four of the law-enforcement officers (as well as Nash) and got away. J. Edgar Hoover began a manhunt to bring the three killers to justice. Although Miller was found dead in a Michigan ditch a few months later, it took more than a year to find Richetti and Floyd. In separate shoot-outs in October 1934, Floyd was killed, and Richetti was captured.

Charles "Pretty Boy" Floyd is shown here on his "Identification Order" poster. Floyd was part of a generation of outlaws in the 1930s whose exploits were so notorious that they became known as "public enemies."

Public Enemy Number One

About the same time, another "public enemy" rose to fame. From May 1933 to July 1934, John Dillinger went on a crime spree. Dillinger and his gang committed bank robberies. People were killed during some of those robberies. When Dillinger was captured, he broke out of jail. When he needed more weapons, he stole them from a police station. Newspapers reported Dillinger's crimes with shock and fear. To some people, he seemed so unstoppable that they came to admire him. J. Edgar Hoover, however, declared Dillinger the greatest menace to society, the worst criminal around: Public Enemy Number One. That title made Dillinger the most wanted man in the United States.

Knowledge of how badly the FBI wanted to catch Dillinger eventually led to his downfall in July 1934. Dillinger was friendly with a woman named Anna Sage. Sage had left her native Romania and lived in the Chicago area. She became a prostitute, ran several houses of prostitution herself, and was now, because of her own problems with the law, facing **deportation** by the U.S. government. Sage offered the FBI a deal. If she could stay in the country, she would lead agents to Dillinger. True to her word, Sage

told the FBI that she would be going to a movie theater with Dillinger. After the show, agents surrounded Dillinger and ordered him to give up. When the criminal reached for a gun, agents shot him down. The FBI was widely praised for putting an end to Dillinger's crime spree.

FAST FACTS

One reason the FBI stopped using the term "Public Enemy Number One" was to prevent criminals from competing to see who was most deserving of the title!

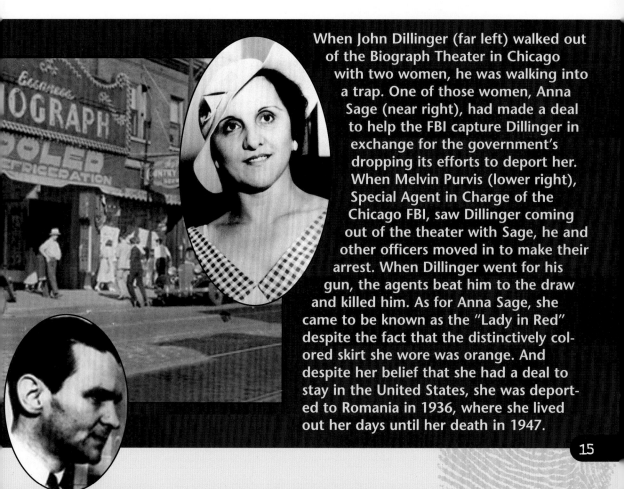

When John Dillinger (far left) walked out of the Biograph Theater in Chicago with two women, he was walking into a trap. One of those women, Anna Sage (near right), had made a deal to help the FBI capture Dillinger in exchange for the government's dropping its efforts to deport her. When Melvin Purvis (lower right), Special Agent in Charge of the Chicago FBI, saw Dillinger coming out of the theater with Sage, he and other officers moved in to make their arrest. When Dillinger went for his gun, the agents beat him to the draw and killed him. As for Anna Sage, she came to be known as the "Lady in Red" despite the fact that the distinctively colored skirt she wore was orange. And despite her belief that she had a deal to stay in the United States, she was deported to Romania in 1936, where she lived out her days until her death in 1947.

Other notorious public enemies of the early 1930s' "gangster era" included (clockwise from left) Bonnie and Clyde, George "Machine Gun" Kelly, Alvin "Creepy" Karpis, and Louis "Lepke" Buchalter. These criminals were ruthless kidnappers, bank robbers, and killers, and the FBI was eager to catch them. Bonnie and Clyde were killed by lawmen, Karpis and Kelly served lengthy prison sentences, and Buchalter was executed by the government.

Other FBI Triumphs—
Bonnie and Clyde

Bonnie Parker and Clyde Barrow led a gang—the Barrow Gang—that robbed banks and committed murders in a crime spree that lasted from 1932 to 1934. The FBI released posters showing their pictures and listing details by which they could be identified. These posters were similar to today's wanted posters. The FBI also played a role in tracking down Bonnie and Clyde to

A crowd gathers to view the bullet-riddled car in which Clyde Barrow and Bonnie Parker were killed by law enforcement officers in Louisiana on May 23, 1934.

Louisiana, where they were killed in a hail of bullets by law enforcement officers lying in wait for them in a roadside ambush.

Machine Gun Kelly

On July 22, 1933, a wealthy oilman named Charles F. Urschel was kidnapped. In a fast-paced and dramatic investigation of the kidnapping, the FBI identified George "Machine Gun" Kelly as one of the kidnappers and tracked him across three states. When FBI agents finally caught Kelly in Memphis, Tennessee, Kelly is said to have begged them, "Don't shoot, G-men! Don't shoot!"

The FBI has since suggested that these were probably not the words Kelly used at the time of his arrest. According to some sources, an agent present at the time of Kelly's arrest was said to have overheard Kelly's wife saying to him, "These G-men will never leave us alone." Whatever the source of the term, and whatever truth to the stories of its being used by Kelly or his wife, the nickname "G-men"—short for "Government Men"—stuck and became part of the popular culture of the time. Alongside the nickname, the image of the G-man as a smart, powerful agent of the law also helped build up the reputation of the FBI in its pursuit of wanted criminals.

CONFLICTING STORIES

As the FBI built up its reputation for catching wanted criminals in the 1930s, J. Edgar Hoover became famous as the Bureau's crime-fighting leader. The stories of his arrests of Alvin "Creepy" Karpis and Louis "Lepke" Buchalter made headlines. Years later, however, when Karpis wrote his autobiography, he said that the story of his arrest by Hoover was not true. According to Karpis, other agents arrested him and made sure he was not armed before Hoover arrived on the scene. Some reports even suggest that when Hoover directed his men to put the cuffs on Karpis, they were forced to use an agent's necktie because, unbeknownst to Hoover, they had not brought handcuffs along. Whoever made the arrest, and however it went down, Karpis himself vouched for one thing: When he saw Hoover, the criminal had no doubt that the FBI had caught him. Karpis wrote of Hoover: ". . . I recognized the dark, heavy man . . . I'd seen pictures of him. Anyone would have known him. . . . I knew at that moment, for sure, that the FBI had finally nailed me."

Famed gossip columnist and radio commentator Walter Winchell's description did not agree with the official FBI description of the Buchalter arrest. According to Winchell, it was he, not Hoover, who met Buchalter on the street corner after arranging for Buchalter to turn himself in. Winchell claims that he then drove Buchalter to meet Hoover, who was parked in a limousine several blocks away.

Creepy Karpis and Louis Lepke

The arrests of Alvin "Creepy" Karpis and Louis "Lepke" Buchalter also gave the FBI major boosts in **publicity**. Karpis was wanted for taking part in many robberies and in the kidnappings of two businessmen. On April 30, 1936, the FBI finally traced him to an apartment building in New Orleans, Louisiana. Agents surrounded the building. According to the FBI, when Karpis and another man came out the building on the morning of May 1, he was personally arrested by J. Edgar Hoover and some of the Director's top aides.

Louis "Lepke" Buchalter (center) is shown being taken to jail while handcuffed to FBI Director J. Edgar Hoover (left).

Hoover was also said to have personally arrested Louis "Lepke" Buchalter on August 24, 1939. Lepke (which means "Little Louis" in Yiddish), was an infamous hit man. As a leader of Murder, Inc., the name the media gave to the organization he ran with other mobsters, notably Meyer Lansky and Benjamin "Bugsy" Siegel, Buchalter provided contract killings, most of them paid for by members of organized crime and carried out against fellow mobsters. He was wanted for these and other crimes by both the state of New York and the federal government.

With New York police closing in on him, Buchalter decided to turn himself in to the FBI because the federal charges against him were less serious. To arrange his surrender, Buchalter contacted Walter Winchell, a radio personality who was a friend of Hoover. According to the FBI, Buchalter then surrendered to Hoover in a meeting on a New York City street corner. It was another triumph for the FBI, and Buchalter became the only major mob leader to be executed by the government for his crimes.

CHAPTER 3 The Ten Most Wanted List

The FBI built its reputation for catching wanted criminals in the 1930s. The publicity that came with catching notorious criminals such as "Creepy" Karpis and "Lepke" Buchalter—not to mention the shoot-out in which FBI agents killed John Dillinger—brought great **prestige** to the FBI. As respect for the Bureau grew, people became willing to work with it. Cooperation from citizens, who provided **tips** about crimes and acted as witnesses, helped the FBI do its job.

Movies such as *The Public Enemy*, which was released in 1931, added to the public image of Bureau "G-men" bringing down the most notorious crooks in the nation.

"Give Me Your Ten Worst"

J. Edgar Hoover was always interested in keeping up public awareness of the FBI—especially its successes. In 1949, he found another way to get publicity for the Bureau. A reporter from the International News Service asked Hoover to "Give me your ten worst . . . the ten toughest guys you would like to capture." The reporter wanted to know the

This is the FBI logbook, its pages tattered and worn, that contained the first Ten Most Wanted list. A close look at the list written in the first column on page one shows that it actually contains 11 entries, not 10. The book, put together in 1950, also has notes and news clippings containing information about the criminals.

names of the 10 criminals the FBI was most eager to catch. The article the reporter wrote was widely read, and, based on its popularity, Hoover developed a new idea. Beginning on March 14, 1950, Hoover announced the names of the first criminals on the FBI's Ten Most Wanted Fugitives list.

First on the list was Thomas James Holden, also known as "Tough Tommy." Holden had a three-decade-long history of crime that included robbing trains, escaping from prison, and murdering his wife. In a **press release**, the FBI declared, "Thomas James Holden is one man whose freedom in society is a menace to every man, woman, and child in America."

The First Ten Most Wanted

Here is the entire first list:

1. **Thomas James Holden**, a murderer, train robber, and jailbreaker.

"Tough Tommy" Holden, first "number one" on the FBI's Most Wanted list.

2. **Morley V. King**, a murderer.

3. **William R. Nesbit**, a jewel thief, murderer, and jailbreaker.

4. **Henry R. Mitchell**, a bank robber.

5. **Omar A. Pinson**, a robber and jailbreaker who had killed a police officer.

Omar Pinson had escaped from prison in 1949 with a cellmate; went on the list in 1950 for five months before being recaptured.

6. **Lee Emory Downs**, an expert safecracker.

Orba Jackson was put on the list after about two and a half years as a prison escapee. He was on the list for only two days before being recaptured.

7. Orba Elmer Jackson, a jailbreaker and postal robber.

8. Glen Roy Wright, an armed robber and jailbreaker.

9. Henry Harland Shetland, a kidnapper and jailbreaker.

10. Morris Guralnick, wanted for stabbing his girlfriend, biting a finger off arresting police officer, and escaping from jail after beating guards with a pipe.

Nine of these 10 men were captured, most after less than a year on the

CAUTION: ARMED AND DANGEROUS

All of the fugitives on the FBI's Ten Most Wanted list are suspected of serious crimes, and the FBI thinks they are dangerous to other members of society. The information that the FBI puts out about fugitives always contains a "Caution" section. In this section, the FBI describes the crimes the fugitive is believed to have committed. Many of the crimes are shocking and brutal. For example, the Wanted poster for Alexis Flores—who was added to the Most Wanted list in May 2007—contains the following information:

CAUTION

ALEXIS FLORES IS WANTED FOR HIS ALLEGED INVOLVEMENT IN THE KIDNAPPING AND MURDER OF A FIVE-YEAR-OLD GIRL IN PHILADELPHIA, PENNSYLVANIA. THE GIRL WAS REPORTED MISSING IN LATE JULY OF 2000, AND LATER FOUND STRANGLED TO DEATH IN A NEARBY APARTMENT IN EARLY AUGUST OF 2000.

Beneath the description of a fugitive's alleged crimes, the FBI always warns that this person is "considered armed and extremely dangerous."

If you see a person you recognize from the Ten Most Wanted list, do not approach him or her. As soon as you can, call the police or your local FBI office. Tell them which fugitive you think you saw, the location, and why you think it was the fugitive. If the information you give leads to an arrest, you may get a reward. In 2008, rewards offered by the FBI for information that leads to the capture of one of the Ten Most Wanted fugitives ranged from $100,000 to $2 million.

list. Henry Mitchell was taken off the list in 1958 after the charges against him were dropped.

Simple Idea, Tough Choices

The main idea behind the Ten Most Wanted Fugitives list program was simple. Hoover wanted to use the power of publicity to help the FBI catch fugitives. Both law enforcement officers and ordinary citizens would be made aware of wanted criminals who were on the loose. The FBI would create posters and other materials that described wanted fugitives. The more people who could recognize a fugitive, the harder it would be for the fugitive to hide.

The standards for deciding which fugitives to put on the Ten Most Wanted list are also simple. According the FBI's Web site, to qualify for the Ten Most Wanted list:

- First, the individual must have a lengthy record of committing serious crimes and/or be considered a particularly dangerous menace to society due to current criminal charges.

- Second, it must be believed that the nationwide publicity afforded by the Program can be of assistance in apprehending the fugitive, who, in turn, should not already be notorious due to other publicity.

The process of selecting fugitives for the Ten Most Wanted list program involves looking at many candidates, and many fugitives meet these standards, so it can be difficult to choose the criminals to put on the list. Each FBI office around the country has lists of fugitives the agents want to catch. First, the FBI's **field offices**—all 56 of them—nominate candidates for the Ten Most Wanted list and give the names to the Criminal Investigative Division (CID) at FBI headquarters. Special agents in the CID and the FBI's Office of Public Affairs choose candidates from these lists and then submit their choices to the assistant director of the CID for approval. Finally, the assistant director of the CID obtains approval from the deputy director of the FBI.

Under Arrest

All these steps in choosing fugitives for the Ten Most Wanted list pay off when fugitives who are on the list are arrested. The Ten Most Wanted list program is highly successful. As of September 2008, a total of 490 fugitives have been listed on the Ten Most Wanted list. Of this group, 460 have been captured—almost 94 percent. More than 150 of the captured fugitives have been caught with the help of ordinary citizens. In many cases, the citizens who help the FBI catch fugitives never become well known. Their names are not given to the **media** to help keep them safe from other criminals who might want to take revenge on them or keep them from further participation in the program.

Once a fugitive on the Most Wanted list is captured, surrenders, or is found dead, he or she is removed from the list, and a new fugitive is listed. Other than capture, surrender, or death, there are only two other ways for a fugitive's name to be taken off the list. If criminal charges against the fugitive are dropped, of course, the wanted person is no longer considered a fugitive. Also, a fugitive is sometimes removed from the list if the FBI no longer thinks the person is

STILL AT LARGE

Victor Manuel Gerena made the Ten Most Wanted list on May 14, 1984. Once Donald Eugene Webb was removed from the list on March 31, 2007, Gerena moved into the position of being on the Ten Most Wanted list longer than any other at-large fugitive currently on the list. He is wanted for a $7 million bank robbery in which he allegedly held hostages at gunpoint and injected them with drugs.

Another longtime Ten Most Wanted Fugitive is James J. "Whitey" Bulger. Bulger has been on the list since 1999, although he was wanted even earlier. He is said to be a leader of an organized crime group whose crimes include 18 murders. In spite of having been profiled many times on the TV show *America's Most Wanted*, Bulger has not been seen since 2002. The FBI is offering a $1 million reward for information leading to the capture of Gerena and a $2 million reward for information leading to the capture of Bulger.

Glen Stewart Godwin actually made the Ten Most Wanted list before Bulger. Godwin is a murderer who escaped from a California prison in 1987. That same year, he was caught and put in prison in Mexico for drug dealing. In 1991, however, he escaped from the Mexican prison. He is said to have murdered another inmate while behind bars in Mexico. The FBI is offering a $100,000 reward for information leading to the capture of Godwin.

FBI TEN MOST WANTED FUGITIVE

BANK ROBBERY; UNLAWFUL FLIGHT TO AVOID PROSECUTION - ARMED ROBBERY; THEFT FROM INTERSTATE SHIPMENT

VICTOR MANUEL GERENA

Photograph taken in 1983   Photograph retouched in 2004   Computer Age Enhanced Photograph

Aliases: Victor Oviz...

FBI TEN MOST WANTED FUGITIVE

RACKETEERING INFLUENCED AND CORRUPT ORGANIZATIONS (RICO) - MURDER (19 COUNTS), CONSPIRACY TO COMMIT MURDER, CONSPIRACY TO COMMIT EXTORTION, NARCOTICS DISTRIBUTION, CONSPIRACY TO COMMIT MONEY LAUNDERING EXTORTION; MONEY LAUNDERING

JAMES J. BULGER

Photograph taken in 1994   Photographs Age Enhanced in 2008

James J. Bulger Video   Additional and Retouched

The FBI is offe... the arrest of Vi...

May 1984
Poster Revised Dec...

FBI TEN MOST WANTED FUGITIVE

UNLAWFUL FLIGHT TO AVOID CONFINEMENT - MURDER, ESCAP...

GLEN STEWART GODWIN

Photograph taken in 1991   Photograph taken in 1991   Age enhanced photograph

Aliases: Michael Carrera, Miguel Carrera, Michael Carmen, Glen Godwin, Glen S. Godwin, Dennis H. McWilliams, Dennis Harold McWilliams

DESCRIPTION

Date of Birth:	June 26, 1958	Hair:	Black/Salt and Pepper
Place of Birth:	Miami, Florida	Eyes:	Green
		Complexion:	Medium to Dark
Height:	6'0"	Sex:	Male
Weight:	200 pounds	Race:	White
Build:	Medium	Nationality:	American
Occupations:	Self-employed in tool supplies, mechanic, construction worker		
Scars and Marks:	None known		

especially dangerous to society. Only six fugitives have ever been taken off the list because the FBI has decided they were no longer dangerous.

To get the word out about wanted fugitives, the FBI issues press releases and posters that describe the fugitive and why he or she is wanted. In the past, it was common to see "Wanted by the FBI" posters in post offices. Today, the FBI also puts this information on its Web site. In some cities, the FBI also puts pictures of fugitives on electronic billboards. In the photo to the right, motorists in Columbus, Ohio, drive past an electronic billboard with the picture of a U.S. marine wanted in the slaying of a pregnant fellow marine in 2008.

COMMUNITY ALERT
Cesar Armando Laurean
21 yrs. old
5'9" 160 lbs.
Wanted for Murder

WANTED

744 2111
Cash Reward

"Wanted by the FBI"

The information about a fugitive that appears on the FBI Web site or on a "Wanted by the FBI" poster is very detailed. At the top of the Web page or poster, the FBI specifies the criminal charges that a fugitive faces. Next comes a photograph, often more than one. To help people identify fugitives who have been on the loose for a long time, the FBI sometimes provides a picture of what artists believe a person would look like after aging a certain number of years. The Web site also offers videos of fugitives and a sound recording of their voices, if any are available.

Beneath the photographs, the FBI lists the **aliases** that the fugitive is known to have used. A detailed description of the fugitive follows. It includes date and place of birth; hair, eye, and complexion color; height, weight, and build; race, sex, and nationality. Also included in this section is a description of any known scars or marks on the fugitive's body. For example, Victor Manuel Gerena, a fugitive who has been on the Most Wanted list since May 1984, is described as having ". . . a one-inch scar and a mole on his right shoulder blade."

Finally, the description includes "remarks" about the fugitive. The FBI has very few remarks about some fugitives. For example, Emigdio Preciado, Jr., who has been on the Most Wanted list since 2007 for the shooting and attempted murder of a Los Angeles County sheriff's deputy, is described as follows: "Preciado is a known member of a violent street gang in Los Angeles, California. He is believed to be in Mexico." About others, however, it gives details about their character traits, likes and dislikes, habits, companions, and possessions—including weapons. The FBI remarks about Robert William Fisher (shown at right), an accused murderer who has been on the Most Wanted list since June 2002, give details about his posture, general physical condition, and interests.

This posting appears on the FBI Web site. It provides examples of the categories of information that one will find on most Ten Most Wanted Fugitive posters.

BY TEN MOST WANTED FUGITIVE

UNLAWFUL FLIGHT TO AVOID PROSECUTION - FIRST DEGREE MURDER (3 COUNTS), ARSON OF AN OCCUPIED STRUCTURE

ROBERT WILLIAM FISHER

Photograph taken in 1999 Photograph taken in 1997

Altered Photographs

Robert William Fisher
Get Realplayer

TRANSCRIPT OF VIDEO

Video tape image depicts Robert William Fisher walking down a street in a residential neighborhood. Fisher is holding a small child and a dog is running around him. Video tape modified and sound removed.

Alias: Robert W. Fisher

DESCRIPTION

Date of Birth:	April 13, 1961		
Place of Birth:	Brooklyn, New York	Hair:	Brown
Height:	6'0"	Eyes:	Blue
Weight:	190 pounds	Complexion:	Light
Build:	Medium	Sex:	Male
Occupations:	Surgical Catheter Technician, Respiratory Therapist, Fireman	Race:	White
		Nationality:	American

Scars and Marks: Fisher has surgical scars on his lower back.

Remarks: Fisher is physically fit and is an avid outdoorsman, hunter, and fisherman. He has a noticeable gold crown on his upper left first bicuspid tooth. He may walk with an exaggerated erect posture and his chest pushed out due to a lower back injury. Fisher is known to chew tobacco heavily. He has ties to New Mexico and Florida. Fisher is believed to be in possession of several weapons, including a high-powered rifle.

CAUTION

ROBERT WILLIAM FISHER IS WANTED FOR ALLEGEDLY KILLING HIS WIFE AND TWO YOUNG CHILDREN AND THEN BLOWING UP THE HOUSE IN WHICH THEY ALL LIVED IN SCOTTSDALE, ARIZONA IN APRIL OF 2001.

CONSIDERED ARMED AND EXTREMELY DANGEROUS

IF YOU HAVE ANY INFORMATION CONCERNING THIS PERSON, PLEASE CONTACT YOUR LOCAL FBI OFFICE OR THE NEAREST

CHAPTER

4 Most Wanted Successes

The FBI had success immediately with the Ten Most Wanted Fugitives program—success that has continued through the years. William R. Nesbit was the first man on the list to be captured.

First Capture

Nesbit was part of a gang of jewel thieves who could not get along with one another. On December 31, 1936, the gang broke into a powderhouse (a place for storing explosives) near Sioux Falls, South Dakota, to steal some dynamite. During the theft, two members of the gang started fighting. One pulled a gun and shot the other to death. The dead man's girlfriend was also part of the gang. When she kneeled down next to the body, another gang member beat her to death. The three remaining gang members—including Nesbit—threw the bodies in the powderhouse and then blew it up. The explosion broke windows 5 miles (8 kilometers) away. Nesbit and the other gang members ran away, but they were all later caught. Nesbit was sentenced to 20 years in prison.

Ten years after the crime, Nesbit escaped from the South Dakota State Penitentiary. He had been on the run for four years when the FBI put him on the Ten Most Wanted list on

March 15, 1950. Once he was put on the list, Nesbit's freedom quickly ended. A boy in Minnesota saw his picture in the newspaper. He thought it looked like a man who lived in a nearby cave. With a few of his friends, the boy went to the cave to get a good look at the man. Seeing that it was Nesbit, they ran to the police. The police hurried to the cave and arrested the wanted fugitive. Nesbit was caught only three days after being put on the list. His capture was the first of many successes of the Ten Most Wanted list.

The Case of the Disappearing Millionaire

Joseph Corbett, Jr., accused of a committing a tragic, widely publicized kidnapping and murder in 1960, is another criminal who was caught after being put on the Ten Most Wanted list.

Joseph Corbett, Jr. (center, wearing glasses), listens to the judge reading the verdict at his trial near Denver, Colorado. Corbett was found guilty in the 1960 murder of Adolph Coors III. He was captured after being placed on the Ten Most Wanted list.

Adolph Coors III was an executive of the famous Coors Brewing Company. On February 9, 1960, his car was found on a small bridge near his Colorado home. Coors himself was missing. The police immediately suspected foul play because they found blood in the car and on the bridge railing. They also found Coors's eyeglasses in the water beneath the bridge. Within a few days, the Coors family received a ransom note. It demanded $500,000 in return for Adolph. The family paid the ransom, but they never saw Adolph again.

Investigators found few clues to help them find out what happened to Coors. All they learned was that people had seen suspicious vehicles near the bridge in the weeks before he disappeared.

On March 30, 1960, the FBI added Joseph Corbett, Jr., to the Ten Most Wanted list. Corbett was a murderer who had escaped from prison five years earlier and was thought to be living near Denver, Colorado.

Although the FBI did not say that Corbett was wanted for the kidnapping, the media put the pieces together. The headline of one newspaper screamed: "FBI Seeking Ex-Convict Coors Case Suspect." One reason the media connected Corbett to the Coors case was that a Denver man using the name Walter Osborne—who turned out to be Corbett—disappeared at about the same time that Coors disappeared. Also, a worker at Coors's home saw a car like Corbett's near where Coors's car was left. The FBI described Corbett as a smart, dangerous killer.

Everyone's worst fears about the case came true in September 1960. A hiker found Coors's bones, clothes, and pocketknife in the Colorado woods. He had been shot. It was not long before the FBI caught up with Corbett. By late October, FBI agents knew he was staying at a hotel in Vancouver, British Columbia, Canada. Some sources say that two Canadians recognized Corbett from a photo in a magazine article by J. Edgar Hoover. Agents and police posed as deliverymen and knocked on Corbett's door. When he opened it, the agents held Corbett at gunpoint and arrested him. He was convicted of murder and sent to prison.

Buried Alive

Another high-profile kidnapping case involving a member of the Ten Most Wanted list had a happier ending than the Coors case. On December 17, 1968, 20-year-old Barbara Jane Mackle became the victim of one of the most terrifying kidnappings anyone ever lived to tell about. Barbara was staying in a hotel in Georgia with her mother. Kidnappers, posing as police officers, came to their hotel room. (Continued on page 36.)

Barbara Jane Mackle, the victim of a terrifying high-profile kidnapping, is shown here decorating a Christmas tree in her home in 1969, one year after she was abducted and placed underground in a coffinlike box. Barbara's kidnappers were captured after being placed on the FBI's Ten Most Wanted List.

RADICALS ON THE RUN

In the 1970s, a new type of fugitive began appearing on the Ten Most Wanted list. During these years, **radical** political groups became more active in the United States. Some members of these groups turned to violent crime in the name of their cause.

On September 4, 1970, J. Edgar Hoover announced four new members of the FBI's Ten Most Wanted Fugitives list: Dwight Alan Armstrong, Karleton Lewis Armstrong, David Sylvan Fine, and Leo Frederick Burt. The four fugitives were members of the New Year's Gang, a group that opposed the Vietnam War. Using a bomb made from fertilizer and fuel oil, the group bombed a building at the University of Wisconsin at Madison.

The building was used in military research. A researcher was killed, and four others were injured. It was the biggest bombing by domestic terrorists before the 1995 Oklahoma City bombing. The Armstrongs and Fine were eventually caught. Burt, however, was never caught. The FBI took him off the Ten Most Wanted List in 1976, but he is still wanted.

According to an FBI spokesperson, radical fugitives could be difficult to catch. The reason for this, the spokesman said, is that

> They have a tendency to go **underground** . . . They have the moral stamina to cut themselves off completely from family and friends, something many criminals won't do.

That was the case with Katherine Ann Power and Susan Edith Saxe, who took part in the robbery of a Boston bank on September 23, 1970. During the robbery, a police officer was shot to death.

By October 17, Power and Saxe were added to the Ten Most Wanted list. Saxe was on the run until she was caught in March 1975. Believing she was hiding near Philadelphia, the FBI had sent out flyers with her picture. A police officer recognized her from the FBI pictures and arrested her. Power was never caught, and in 1984, the FBI took her off the Ten Most Wanted List. In 1993, however, Power turned herself in. After 23 years on the run, she was suffering under the stress of living under a false identity. Power served six years in prison and was released in 1999.

WANTED WANTED BY THE FBI

TAGE; DESTRUCTION OF GOVERNMENT PI
CONSPIRACY
DAVID SYLVAN FINE

SABOTAGE; DESTRUCTION OF GOVERNMENT PROPERTY;
CONSPIRACY
KARLETON LEWIS ARMSTRONG

ANTED BY T
FB
AGE; DESTRUCTION OF GOVERNMENT PROPER
CONSPIRACY
WIGHT ALAN ARMSTRONG

WANTED BY T FB
SABOTAGE; DESTRUCTION OF GOVERNMENT PROPERTY
CONSPIRACY
LEO FREDERICK BURT

In the 1960s, Sterling Hall, on the campus of the University of Wisconsin at Madison, housed the Army Mathematics Research Center. A focus of opposition to the war in Vietnam, the building was bombed in 1970. Following the bombing, which killed a researcher not connected to the military, the four men responsible for the blast (upper left) were placed on the FBI's Most Wanted Fugitives list. Three were caught. The fourth, Leo Burt, remains at large. He is shown at lower left in a series of retouched photos to show possible signs of aging.

WANTED
BY THE FBI

SABOTAGE; DESTRUCTION OF GOVERNMENT PROPERTY;
CONSPIRACY
LEO FREDERICK BURT

Photograph taken in 1969   Photographic retouch

Eugene Donald Fieldston

DESCRIPTION

irth Used:	April 18, 1948; April 15, 1950	**Hair:**	Brown (may now be gray)
irth:	Darby, Pennsylvania	**Eyes:**	Hazel
	5'11" to 6'0"	**Sex:**	Male
	185 pounds	**Race:**	White
	W735004020	**Nationality:**	American
as:	Laborer and watchman		
Marks:	None known		

Burt may wear a moustache and beard and has worn his hair long in the back. He may also wear glasses. Burt has ties to New York City, New York; Boston, Massachusetts; and Peterborough, Ontario, Canada.

CAUTION

k Burt is wanted for allegedly participating in the bombing of Sterling Hall, on
f the University of Wisconsin, on August 24, 1970. The blast from the
mbined with the fire, resulted in the death of a 33-year-old researcher.
there were several injuries

WANTED
BY THE FBI

INTERSTATE FLIGHT - MURDER;
THEFT OF GOVERNMENT PROPERTY
SUSAN EDITH SAXE

FBI No. 545,575 H

Radicals Susan Edith Saxe (above) and Katherine Ann Power (left) were also placed on the Most Wanted list in 1970 following their involvement in a bank robbery in Boston in which one of their **accomplices** shot and killed a police officer.

35

They tied up Barbara's mother and took Barbara prisoner. They drove her into the woods, where they forced her into a special grave they had set up with food, water, and a pipe to bring in air. The kidnappers said they were going to leave her in the grave unless her father paid the ransom they wanted. If he paid, they would reveal where she was buried. If he did not, they would leave Barbara to die.

The kidnappers then called Barbara's parents and demanded money—$500,000 in $20 bills. Robert Mackle was a wealthy man, and he had enough money to pay the ransom. By the time the kidnappers demanded the ransom, though, the Mackles had already called the FBI. Working with the FBI, the Mackles planned to follow the kidnappers' directions while FBI agents watched to see who picked up the money.

Things did not, however, go as planned. Two Florida police-men who did not know what was going on accidentally dis-rupted the ransom drop-off. The kidnappers fled, but they left behind their getaway car. Finding the car was a big break in the case. In the car, agents found all the information they needed to tell them exactly whom they needed to catch: a couple named Gary Steven Krist and Ruth Eisemann-Schier.

Krist called the Mackles to set up another ransom drop-off. On the second try, he got away with the money. Then he called the FBI office in Atlanta, Georgia, and revealed where Barbara was buried. More than 100 agents rushed into the woods to rescue her. They quickly found where Barbara was buried and freed her. Incredibly, she was all right.

The kidnappers were on the run. The story of Barbara's ordeal was big news, and Gary Krist was added to the FBI's Ten Most Wanted Fugitives list on December 20, 1968. Part

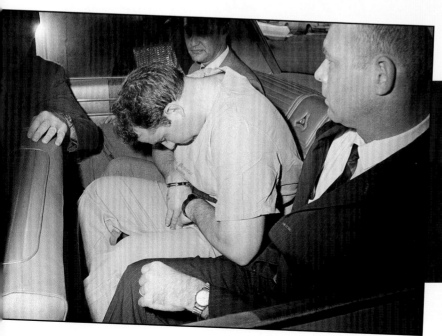

Gary Steven Krist is shown being taken by FBI agents from a Florida hospital. Krist had been suffering from exhaustion and exposure prior to his capture.

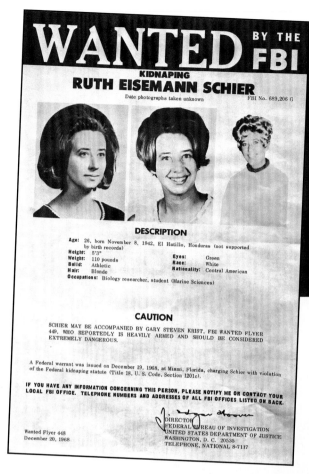

WANTED BY THE FBI

KIDNAPING
RUTH EISEMANN SCHIER
Date photographs taken unknown

FBI No. 689,206 G

DESCRIPTION

Age: 26, born November 8, 1942, El Hatillo, Honduras (not supported by birth records)
Height: 5'3"
Weight: 110 pounds
Build: Athletic
Hair: Blonde
Eyes: Green
Race: White
Nationality: Central American
Occupations: Biology researcher, student (Marine Sciences)

CAUTION

SCHIER MAY BE ACCOMPANIED BY GARY STEVEN KRIST, FBI WANTED FLYER 449, WHO REPORTEDLY IS HEAVILY ARMED AND SHOULD BE CONSIDERED EXTREMELY DANGEROUS.

A Federal warrant was issued on December 19, 1968, at Miami, Florida, charging Schier with violation of the Federal kidnaping statute (Title 18, U. S. Code, Section 1201c).

IF YOU HAVE ANY INFORMATION CONCERNING THIS PERSON, PLEASE NOTIFY ME OR CONTACT YOUR LOCAL FBI OFFICE. TELEPHONE NUMBERS AND ADDRESSES OF ALL FBI OFFICES LISTED ON BACK.

DIRECTOR
FEDERAL BUREAU OF INVESTIGATION
UNITED STATES DEPARTMENT OF JUSTICE
WASHINGTON, D. C. 20535
TELEPHONE, NATIONAL 8-7117

Wanted Flyer 448
December 20, 1968

Ruth Eisemann-Schier is shown here on the poster that marked the first time a woman had made the Most Wanted list. She had separated from Gary Steven Krist during the botched delivery of Barbara Jane Mackle's ransom and managed to stay on the loose for about two and a half months longer than Krist before being traced through her fingerprints.

of the credit for Krist's capture goes to Norman Oliphant, who sold Krist the boat in which he tried to flee with the ransom money. Oliphant suspected that the man who paid for the boat with a stack of $20 bills was the wanted criminal Gary Krist. Oliphant called the police immediately.

On December 22, Krist was captured after a dramatic helicopter and boat chase. He was caught with the ransom money. Eisemann-Schier, however, had vanished—but not for long.

On December 28, she was added to the Ten Most Wanted Fugitives list. Eisemann-Schier became the first woman ever to make the list. By early March 1969, she was also captured. When she applied for a job at a state hospital in Oklahoma, her fingerprints gave her away as a wanted criminal.

CHAPTER 5 The Ten Most Wanted in the Media

Ever since J. Edgar Hoover announced the Ten Most Wanted Fugitives list, the FBI has used the power of the media to help catch criminal suspects. Beginning in the 1960s, television programs have also helped get the word out about wanted fugitives. With many viewers watching these shows, it became much harder to be a fugitive. In addition to television shows, Web sites and radio spots also provide people with information about fugitives.

The FBI

The FBI was a television drama that was on the air from 1965 to 1974. The main character, Inspector Lewis Erskine, was played by actor Efrem

Efrem Zimbalist, Jr., is shown here in the role of Inspector Lewis Erskine in *The FBI*. Each show was carefully reviewed by Director J. Edgar Hoover, who often voiced strong opinions not only about the show's content, but about the political leanings of some of the guest stars.

Zimbalist, Jr. Some of the stories of the show's weekly episodes were based on real FBI cases. The actual FBI played a role in making the show. J. Edgar Hoover gave his personal approval for each episode, and the Bureau gave the show's producers advice about FBI procedures.

At the end of each episode of *The FBI*, Zimbalist gave a short presentation about a real fugitive whom the FBI was trying to catch. After one 1968 episode, Zimbalist alerted viewers that the FBI was after James Earl Ray for the assassination of civil rights leader Martin Luther King, Jr. Ray was put on the Ten Most Wanted Fugitives list on April 20, 1968, and was captured on June 8.

In March 1969, Zimbalist told viewers about a very dangerous fugitive named Richard Lee Tingler. Tingler had been added to the Ten Most Wanted Fugitives list on December 20,

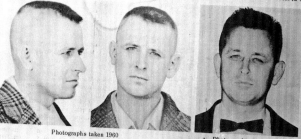

WANTED BY THE **FBI**

CIVIL RIGHTS - CONSPIRACY
INTERSTATE FLIGHT - ROBBERY
JAMES EARL RAY　　FBI No. 405,942 G

Photographs taken 1960

Photograph taken 1968
(eyes drawn by artist)

Aliases: Eric Starvo Galt, W. C. Herron, Harvey Lowmyer, James McBride, James O'Conner, James Walton, James Walyon, John Willard, "Jim,"

DESCRIPTION

Age:	40, born March 10, 1928, at Quincy or Alton, Illinois (not supported by birth records)		
Height:	5' 10"		
Weight:	163 to 174 pounds	**Eyes:**	Blue
Build:	Medium	**Complexion:**	Medium
Hair:	Brown, possibly cut short	**Race:**	White
Occupations:	Baker, color matcher, laborer	**Nationality:**	American

Scars and Marks: Small scar on center of forehead and small scar on palm of right hand
Remarks: Noticeably protruding left ear; reportedly is a lone wolf; allegedly attended dance instruction school; has reportedly completed course in bartending.
Fingerprint Classification: 16 M 9 U OOO 12
　　　　　　　　　　　　　M 4 W I O I

CRIMINAL RECORD

Ray has been convicted of burglary, robbery, forging U. S. Postal Money Orders, armed robbery, and operating motor vehicle without owner's consent.

CAUTION

SOUGHT IN CONNECTION WITH A MURDER WHEREIN THE VICTIM WAS SHOT. CONSIDER AND EXTREMELY DANGEROUS.

A Federal warrant was issued on April 17, 1968, at Birmingham, Alabama, charging Ray as Eric Starvo Galt with conspiring to interfere with a Constitutional Right of a citizen (Title 18, U. S. Code, Section 241). A Federal warrant was also issued on July 20, 1967 Interstate Flight to A

In 1968, Efrem Zimbalist, Jr., put viewers of *The FBI* on alert that James Earl Ray had been placed on the Ten Most Wanted Fugitives list for the assassination of Martin Luther King, Jr. *The FBI*'s producers frequently clashed with J. Edgar Hoover over the content of the program. Although Hoover reportedly felt **animosity** toward King, the segment on Ray was permitted to air.

1968. Three months before, on October 20, a gunman robbed a dairy store in Columbus, Ohio, and murdered two employees. A third employee survived the attack and identified Tingler as the person responsible. Tingler—who had a long history of crime and had already served time in prison—was already known to police. Authorities investigating the dairy store murders then connected Tingler to four murders that had been committed in Cleveland the previous month. The FBI sent out information about Tingler, even warning people that he might disguise himself as a woman.

FAST FACTS

James Earl Ray—the killer of civil rights leader Martin Luther King, Jr.—made the FBI's Ten Most Wanted Fugitives list twice. He was put on the list the first time because of the **assassination** and was caught after about two months. He was put on the list the second time after he escaped from prison. This time, he was caught after two days.

Shortly after Tingler was profiled on *The FBI*, an Oklahoma farmer noticed that one of his new employees, Don Williams, had become nervous. He reported Williams to the police, who contacted the FBI. It turned out that Don Williams was really Richard Lee Tingler. He was arrested in May 1969.

America's Most Wanted

On February 7, 1988, a new TV show called *America's Most Wanted* premiered on the FOX network. It is no ordinary drama or sitcom. The host of the show is John Walsh. Walsh has a deep personal connection to crime victims. In 1981, his six-year-old son, Adam, was kidnapped and murdered. After Adam's murder, Walsh dedicated his life to helping families with missing children as well as all types of crime victims. In his book *Public Enemies*, Walsh writes: "In Adam's memory, I did everything I could to try to help all the other children who would go missing. I have made it my life's work, and it is how I make sure that Adam did not die in vain." FOX chose him to host *America's Most Wanted* because of his reputation for helping crime victims and their families and his passion for justice.

Each episode of *America's Most Wanted* profiles some of the most wanted fugitives in the United States— including members of the FBI's

John Walsh (left) is shown speaking on a publicity tour for the show he hosts, *America's Most Wanted*. When his son Adam (right) was kidnapped and murdered in 1981, Walsh devoted his life to preventing similar tragedies from happening to other kids. His work led to the development of *America's Most Wanted* in 1988.

"WATCH TELEVISION. CATCH FUGITIVES."

When the show began, the slogan for *America's Most Wanted* was "Watch television. Catch fugitives." The show began having results almost immediately. The first episode of *America's Most Wanted* featured a profile of David James Roberts. Roberts was a convicted murderer who had escaped from prison in Indiana in the late 1960s. He had been on the FBI's Ten Most Wanted Fugitives list since April 27, 1987. Right after he was profiled on *America's Most Wanted*, people began calling in to the show's hotline with tips. Many people said that Roberts looked a lot like a man named Bob Lord, who ran a homeless shelter in Staten Island, New York. Even Lord's girlfriend called in. She said that Lord was sick and in the hospital. When police arrived at the hospital, they found that the man who called himself Bob Lord had suddenly checked out. He had apparently seen a copy of *TV Guide*, which said that Roberts would be featured on *America's Most Wanted*. Four days after the first episode aired, police found him hiding in Staten Island.

The next year, *America's Most Wanted* profiled several fugitives who were on the FBI's Ten Most Wanted list. Many of these fugitives were captured with the help of the show's viewers. For example, on September 28, 1989, *America's Most Wanted* received a tip that Pedro Luis Estrada was living in a house in Harrisburg, Pennsylvania. Estrada was a former professional boxer who was charged with seven counts of murder. *America's Most Wanted* gave the tip to the FBI. Agents watched the house until they were sure the man there was Estrada. Then, on October 1, FBI agents and a **SWAT** team took Estrada by surprise as he left the house and easily arrested him.

America's Most Wanted has even led to the capture of criminals who had fled the United States. In August 2008, the show again helped the FBI net one of the Ten Most Wanted Fugitives. FBI Director Robert Mueller had appeared on the show in July to announce that Michael Jason Registe had been added to the Ten Most Wanted Fugitives list. Registe was suspected of murdering two Georgia college students. Soon after *America's Most Wanted* profiled Registe, tips came in that the wanted man was on St. Maarten, a small island in the Caribbean. Police on the island found Registe and arrested him on August 27.

FBI TEN MOST WANTED FUGITIVE
UNLAWFUL FLIGHT TO AVOID PROSECUTION - MURDER
MICHAEL JASON REGISTE

Ten Most Wanted Fugitives list. The show features interviews with crime victims and investigators, **re-enactments** of crimes, displays of evidence, and visits to crime scenes. The show's most important feature, however, are the pictures it displays of crime suspects who have not yet been caught. Like the FBI's Ten Most

FAST FACTS

In 1996, FOX was about to cancel *America's Most Wanted*, but governors, law enforcement officials, and viewers insisted on keeping the show on the air.

Wanted Fugitives list, the goal of *America's Most Wanted* is to use publicity to help catch fugitives from the law. The show runs a **hotline** that viewers can call if they have seen a fugitive. *America's Most Wanted* has been very effective. As of October 2008, the show had played a role in the capture of 1,040 fugitives. Sixteen of the fugitives caught with the help of *America's Most Wanted* have been on the FBI's Ten Most Wanted list.

Other Media Outlets

In addition to *America's Most Wanted*, the TV show *Unsolved Mysteries* has also described fugitives from the FBI's Ten Most Wanted list. The show was on the air from 1987 to 2002. After several years off the air, *Unsolved Mysteries* returned in October 2008.

Television shows, however, are not the only medium that is used to get the word out about who is on the FBI's Ten Most Wanted Fugitives list. Since 1996, the FBI has listed the Ten Most Wanted Fugitives on its Web site. That helped lead to the

CAPTURED

WANTED BY THE FBI
Leslie Isben Rogge

Bank Robbery; Interstate Transportation of Stolen Property;
Fraud by Wire

CAPTURED

Isben Rogge
s taken 1989

Escaped bank robber
Leslie Isben Rogge became the first
"success" story of the FBI's decision to put its Ten
Most Wanted Fugitives program online. Rogge
had fled to Guatemala, and when a 14-year-old
neighbor recognized him from the postings on
the Internet, he notified Guatemalan authorities.
With the police on his tail, Rogge turned himself
in to U.S. officials in Guatemala.

capture of Leslie Isben Rogge, an escaped bank robber who had fled to Guatemala. Someone who knew Rogge saw him listed on the FBI Web site and tipped off the Guatemalan National Police that Rogge was in their country. With the Guatemalan police after him, Rogge turned himself in at the U.S. embassy in Guatemala.

America's Most Wanted also has an active Web site that provides information about a wide variety of fugitives and missing persons. In addition, the ABC News Web site features a section called "Fugitive Watch." Both the FBI and *America's Most Wanted* use email to alert people about fugitives and other missing persons. *America's Most Wanted* also broadcasts a radio show on the ABC Radio Network.

Even comics have been used to help catch wanted fugitives. In 1999, the Dick Tracy detective comic strip included profiles of the criminals then on the Ten Most Wanted list. The profiles included with these comics even led to the capture of a fugitive.

CATCHING A MAN ON THE RUN

Among the criminals that *America's Most Wanted* featured was Warren Steed Jeffs (top right). Jeffs was the leader of a religious **sect** that was believed to force girls as young as 13 years old to get married to adult members of the group. Many of these men had many wives. Members of the sect thought of Jeffs as a prophet and were almost completely under his control.

On June 9, 2005, Jeffs was charged in Arizona with crimes including sexual conduct with a minor and rape as an accomplice. But Jeffs was on the run and authorities could not find him. Eventually, on May 6, 2006, the FBI added Jeffs to its Ten Most Wanted Fugitives. The same day, he was featured on *America's Most Wanted*.

On August 29, near Las Vegas, Nevada State Highway Patrol trooper Eddie Dutchover stopped a car because it had no visible identification. Dutchover spoke to the three people inside and became suspicious. The tall, thin man in the back was very nervous. Dutchover suspected that the man was Warren Steed Jeffs. When two more troopers arrived and began searching the vehicle, Dutchover's suspicions were confirmed. The troopers found letters addressed to Jeffs, as well as $54,000 in cash, 15 cell phones, laptop computers, walkie-talkies, a police scanner, credit cards, sunglasses, and wigs. After the troopers called in backup officers and FBI agents, the man admitted his identity.

The arrest of Jeffs was another victory for the FBI and its Ten Most Wanted Fugitives list, as well as *America's Most Wanted*.

In 1999, *Dick Tracy's* "Crimestoppers Textbook" had become a miniature gallery for the FBI's Ten Most Wanted. The men shown here are still on the list and are featured in this book on page 26.

CHAPTER 6 Most Wanted Terrorists

From bank robbers to murderers to kidnappers to mobsters, the FBI's Ten Most Wanted Fugitives list has always included a wide variety of criminal suspects. In the 1970s, some members of radical groups who committed bombings in support of their political beliefs made the list. Beginning in the 1990s, however, terrorists—people who use violence to scare others into going along with their political views—became more common on the Ten Most Wanted Fugitives list. After the September 11, 2001, terrorist attacks on the United States, the FBI created a separate Most Wanted list for terrorists.

The explosion of Pan Am Flight 103 over Lockerbie, Scotland, in 1988, was part of an era of international terror that would **culminate** in the attacks of 9/11.

47

The Bombing of Pan Am Flight 103

Among the first fugitives who made the Ten Most Wanted list on charges of terrorism were Abdel Basset Ali al-Megrahi and Al Amin Khalifah Fhimah. They were wanted for the bombing of Pan Am Flight 103. On December 21, 1988, a bomb tore a hole in the side of a Boeing 747 jet traveling from London, England, to New York City. The plane went down over Lockerbie, Scotland. A total of 270 people died in the crash—all 259 people on the plane, plus 11 people on the ground. Investigators—including FBI explosives experts—rushed to Lockerbie.

FAST FACTS

Two Americans are on the Most Wanted Terrorists list. Al-Qaeda member Adam Yahiye Gadahn is wanted for treason. Animal-rights extremist Daniel Andreas San Diego is wanted for bombing business offices.

After a huge effort, they figured out that a small, powerful bomb had been wrapped in clothes and hidden in a suitcase. Evidence pointed to al-Megrahi and Fhimah as the bombers. Al-Megrahi was an agent of the government of Libya; Fhimah had been a manager for Libyan Arab Airlines. The two men were added to the FBI's Ten Most Wanted Fugitives list on March 23, 1995. Law enforcement, however, could not act against the men because they were being protected by the Libyan government. Eventually, **economic sanctions** forced Libya to turn them in, and the men were put on trial. Al-Megrahi was found guilty of the bombing, while Fhimah was acquitted.

Ramzi Yousef masterminded the first bombing of the World Trade Center in New York City, in February 1993. Placed on the FBI's Ten Most Wanted Fugitives list that same year, Yousef was eventually turned in by a man he had hoped would help him plan another attack. The man had learned of the FBI's $2 million reward, however, and he turned Yousef in to U.S. authorities in Pakistan.

The Truck Bomb at the World Trade Center

Another Ten Most Wanted Fugitive wanted for terrorism charges was Ramzi Yousef. Yousef led a group of terrorists who built a huge bomb. On February 26, 1993, they hid the bomb in a truck and parked the truck in the garage beneath the South Tower of the World Trade Center in New York City. The explosion killed six people, injured about 1,000 others, and did a lot of damage to the building.

The FBI, the New York City Police Department, and other law enforcement agencies quickly found and arrested several of the terrorists involved in the bombing. Yousef, however, was a smart and very dangerous terrorist. He left the United States as soon as he could. Papers found in the house where the terrorists made the bomb told the FBI that Yousef played a major role in the plot. He was hard to find, though, because not much was known about him. The FBI put Yousef on the Ten Most Wanted Fugitives list on April 21, 1993, and announced a $2 million reward for information leading to his capture.

49

To get the word out that he was wanted, the U.S. State Department put information about Yousef on matchbooks and spread them around Pakistan and Central Asia. Authorities made little progress in finding Yousef, though, until he made a mistake. While building a bomb in the Philippines, Yousef accidentally started a fire in an apartment. He fled to Pakistan, but he left behind key evidence: his laptop computer. When police read what was in the laptop, they realized that Yousef was plotting major bombings and assassinations.

Yousef's luck soon ran out. In Pakistan, he tried to get a man named Istaique Parker to help him in another plot. Parker, however, knew that Yousef was wanted—and that he could get a reward for turning Yousef in. Parker contacted the U.S. Embassy, and Yousef was arrested

Investigators dig through the rubble of the bombing of the World Trade Center in 1993. Explosives were placed in the garage beneath the Twin Towers. As this photo shows, damage was extensive.

DOMESTIC TERRORISTS

Not all terrorists who have been on the Ten Most Wanted Fugitives list are from foreign countries. Eric Robert Rudolph and Clayton Lee Waagner are both Americans who terrorized other Americans. Both of these terrorists had similar motivation: They oppose abortion. Their crimes, however, were different.

In the late 1990s, Rudolph planted several bombs, including two at women's health clinics and one at Centennial Park, in Atlanta, Georgia, that went off during the 1996 Olympics. Rudolph was living in the North Carolina mountains when the FBI got a tip in 1998 that connected him to one of the clinic bombings. The FBI sent hundreds of agents to look for Rudolph, but the fugitive had disappeared. Five years later, in 2003, a young police officer stopped a man acting suspiciously in an alley behind a grocery. A second officer who arrived on the scene recognized the man as Rudolph. Rudolph is now serving a life sentence in a maximum-security prison.

Clayton Lee Waagner was an escaped convict who was a member of a militant anti-abortion group. He took advantage of the tense mood in the United States after letters containing the dangerous substance anthrax were mailed to people in September and October 2001. Early in November, Waagner sent out 550 envelopes to abortion-rights organizations and clinics. In the envelopes were white powder and a note that read, "You have been exposed to anthrax. We are going to kill all of you." Waagner's envelopes were a **hoax**: The white powder was not dangerous. The hoax, however, caused a great scare amid the real anthrax attacks.

On September 21, 2001—even before his anthrax hoax—Waagner had been added to the Ten Most Wanted Fugitives list. He was already known for threatening abortion-rights supporters, and he was also suspected in bank robberies and vehicle thefts. About one month after his anthrax hoax, Waagner was in a Kinko's store using a computer. An alert clerk recognized him and called 911, leading to his arrest.

on February 7, 1995. According to John Miller and Michael Stone, who wrote *The Cell*, a book about terrorist plots against the United States:

> On the flight to the U.S., Yousef couldn't help boasting to agents about his exploits, even drawing a diagram of where he placed the bomb under the South Tower in the garage. He'd hoped, he told the agents, that it would topple "like a tree" into its twin, resulting, he'd calculated, in 125,000 deaths.

Yousef was put on trial and convicted. Today, he is serving a life sentence in a U.S. maximum-security prison.

The Most Wanted Terrorists List

Osama bin Laden became **infamous** around the world as the leader of al-Qaeda, the Muslim extremist group behind the September 11, 2001, attacks on the United States. Long before that date, however, bin Laden's terrorist group had been attacking Americans overseas. Al-Qaeda played a role in a 1993 attack on American troops in Somalia. In 1998, al-Qaeda attacked the U.S. embassies in Dar es Salaam, Tanzania, and Nairobi, Kenya. These simultaneous attacks took more than 250 lives. On June 7, 1999, the FBI added bin Laden to the Ten Most Wanted Fugitives list. He was wanted for his role in the embassy bombings. In 2000, al-Qaeda attacked a U.S. naval destroyer, the USS *Cole*, killing 17 U.S. sailors.

Bin Laden's worst, however, was yet to come. The next year, on September 11, al-Qaeda members hijacked four

Osama bin Laden's Most Wanted poster was first placed on the FBI's Web site in 1999. After the attacks of September 11, 2001, which were carried out by bin Laden's extremist group, the FBI created a new category, Most Wanted Terrorists.

MURDER OF U.S. NATIONALS OUTSIDE THE UNITED STATES; CONSPIRACY TO MURDER U.S. NATIONALS OUTSIDE THE UNITED STATES; ATTACK ON A FEDERAL FACILITY RESULTING IN DEATH

USAMA BIN LADEN

Aliases: Usama Bin Muhammad Bin Ladin, Shaykh Usama Bin Ladin, The Prince, The Emir, Abu Abdallah, Mujahid Shaykh, Hajj, The Director

DESCRIPTION

Date of Birth Used:	1957		
Place of Birth:	Saudi Arabia	**Hair:**	Brown
Height:	6'4" to 6'6"	**Eyes:**	Brown
Weight:	Approximately 160 pounds	**Sex:**	Male
Build:	Thin	**Complexion:**	Olive
Language:	Arabic (probably Pashtu)	**Citizenship:**	Saudi Arabian
Scars and Marks:	None known		
Remarks:	Bin Laden is left-handed and walks with a cane.		

CAUTION

Usama Bin Laden is wanted in connection with the August 7, 1998, bombings of the United States Embassies in Dar es Salaam, Tanzania, and Nairobi, Kenya. These attacks killed over 200 people. In addition, Bin Laden is a suspect in other terrorist attacks throughout the world.

REWARD

The Rewards For Justice Program, United States Department of State, is offering a reward of up to $25 million for information leading directly to the apprehension or conviction of Usama Bin Laden. An additional $2 million is being offered through a program developed and funded by the Airline Pilots Association and the Air Transport Association.

SHOULD BE CONSIDERED ARMED AND DANGEROUS

IF YOU HAVE ANY INFORMATION CONCERNING THIS PERSON, PLEASE CONTACT YOUR LOCAL FBI OFFICE OR THE NEAREST AMERICAN EMBASSY OR CONSULATE.

jetliners. The hijackers crashed two of them into the Twin Towers of the World Trade Center and one into the Pentagon, which is in Virginia just outside of Washington, D.C. (Passengers and crew on the fourth plane, alerted by people on the ground to the other attacks, fought heroically with the hijackers and caused the plane to crash into a field in Pennsylvania. It is believed that the hijackers intended to crash that plane into a target in Washington, possibly the White House or the Capitol.)

All passengers and crew aboard the planes were killed, along with many people in the Twin Towers and the Pentagon. Almost 3,000 people died in the attacks. Bin Laden instantly became the world's most wanted terrorist. To find

The second of two passenger jets that were crashed into the World Trade Center on September 11, 2001, is shown an instant before impact. Since the events of 9/11, the FBI has reassessed its response to terrorist threats from inside and outside the nation.

him, the United States led an international coalition that invaded Afghanistan, the country that was protecting bin Laden and al-Qaeda. As of 2009, bin Laden and many of his top aides remained on the loose, in spite of huge rewards for tips leading to their capture. In early 2009, President Barack Obama announced his intention to increase the U.S. military presence in Afghanistan in an effort to find bin Laden and further weaken al-Qaeda's presence in that country and neighboring Pakistan.

Shortly after the events of September 11, 2001, the FBI created a special Most Wanted list for terrorists. Speaking at FBI headquarters on October 10, President George W. Bush announced the first 22 Most Wanted Terrorists:

The men on the wall here have put themselves on the list because of great acts of evil. . . . These 22 individuals do not account for all the terrorist activity in the world, but they're among the most dangerous: the leaders and key supporters, the planners and strategists. They must be found; they will be stopped; and they will be punished.

This effort is part of a worldwide assault on terror. All our allies and friends will now be familiar with these evildoers and their associates. For those who join our coalition, we expect results. And a good place to start— help us bring these folks to justice.

The terrorist suspects on the list were wanted for attacks that included the 1993 World Trade Center bombing, the 1998 U.S. embassy bombings, and the bombing of the USS

On October 12, 2000, al-Qaeda suicide bombers sailed up to the USS *Cole* in the port of Aden, Yemen, blowing a hole in its side and killing 17 U.S. sailors. Since the 1990s, various attacks on U.S. citizens and property around the world have been linked to al-Qaeda.

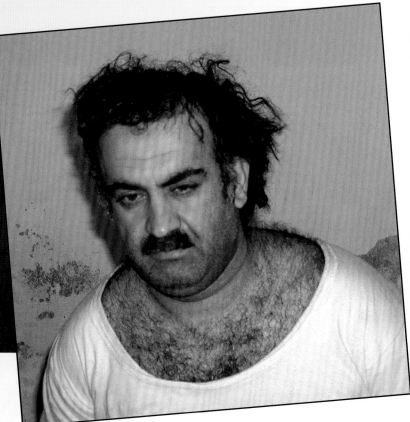

Khalid Shaikh Mohammed, the alleged mastermind behind the attacks of September 11, is shown shortly after his arrest in 2003 in Pakistan. Even before 9/11, Mohammed had been involved in various plots against the United States.

Cole. The FBI says that some of these terrorists may face more charges for the attacks of September 11, 2001. Among the Most Wanted Terrorists who have been captured is Khalid Shaikh Mohammed. Mohammed worked with Ramzi Yousef on a plot to blow up U.S. airplanes, and he also took part in the planning of the September 11 attacks. He was captured in Pakistan on March 1, 2003.

The FBI continues to use both the Most Wanted Terrorists list and the Ten Most Wanted Fugitives list to serve and protect the American people as well as those from other countries who are visiting or working in the United States or in U.S. offices abroad.

CHRONOLOGY

1870: The U.S. Department of Justice is created.

1908: U.S. Attorney General Charles J. Bonaparte creates an unnamed force of "special agents" in the Department of Justice.

1909: The force of "special agents" is named the Bureau of Investigation.

1919: The Bureau issues "Identification Order Number 1" for William N. Bishop, an escaped military prisoner. Bishop has become, in effect, the subject of the Bureau's first Wanted poster.

1924: J. Edgar Hoover becomes director of the Bureau.

1932: The child of Charles and Anne Morrow Lindbergh is kidnapped and later found murdered in New Jersey.

1934: Bruno Hauptmann is captured, charged, and convicted in the kidnap and murder of the Lindbergh baby.

Hoover names John Dillinger "Public Enemy Number One"; Dillinger is killed by agents in July.

1950: The Ten Most Wanted Fugitives list is founded on March 14; William R. Nesbit is the first fugitive from the list to be captured.

1952: Bank robber Willie Sutton is captured after he is recognized from the Ten Most Wanted list.

1965: *The FBI* debuts on television and airs until 1974.

1968: *The FBI* TV series includes a segment about James Earl Ray, wanted for the assassination of Martin Luther King, Jr.

Ruth Eisemann-Schier becomes the first woman on the Ten Most Wanted Fugitives list.

1969: Billie Austin Bryant is captured on January 8 after only two hours on the Ten Most Wanted list.

1988: *America's Most Wanted* debuts on television on February 7.

1993: Ramzi Yousef is put on the Ten Most Wanted Fugitives list on April 21 for the February 23 bombing of the World Trade Center in New York City.

1995: Abdel Basset Ali al-Megrahi and Al Amin Khalifah Fhimah are added to the FBI's Ten Most Wanted Fugitives list on March 23 for the 1988 bombing of Pan Am Flight 103.

1996: The Ten Most Wanted Fugitives list is first posted on the FBI's Web site.

1999: Osama bin Laden is added to the Ten Most Wanted Fugitives list for his role in the bombings of two U.S. embassies in Africa.

2001: The Most Wanted Terrorists list is created in October in the aftermath of the September 11 attacks on the United States.

2009: Animal-rights extremist Daniel Andreas San Diego, wanted for bomb attacks on two corporate offices, becomes the first domestic U.S. terrorist on the FBI's Most Wanted Terrorists list.

GLOSSARY

accomplice—a person who helps someone else commit a crime.

alias—a false name.

animosity—intense dislike or hostility.

assassination—a murder, especially for a political reason.

autobiography—a book about a person's life written by that person.

culminate—to reach a climax or high point of development.

deportation—the process of expelling a person from a country, usually by returning that person to the foreign country from which he or she came.

economic sanctions—government policies banning trade with a certain country in order to put pressure on that country.

field office—an FBI office in a city other than Washington, D.C.

fugitive—a person who is running away, especially someone who is trying to escape from the law.

hoax—an act intended to make people believe something that is not true.

hotline—a telephone number set up so that members of the public can make direct, immediate contact with a special service.

infamous—well known for doing bad things.

media—sources of information that reach many people at once, such as newspapers, radio, and television.

notorious—widely known, especially for something bad.

press release—an official statement giving information to the media.

prestige—high status in people's minds.

profile—a list of the main features and traits of a person.

publicity—activity that increases public attention and interest in a matter.

radical—a person who wants to make extreme changes in society.

ransom—money demanded for the release of someone who is being held captive.

re-enactment—the process of acting out a scene or incident.

sect—a religious group with beliefs and practices that are different from those of more established groups.

Secret Service—the division of the U.S. Treasury Department whose main function is protecting the president, the vice president, and their families.

sect—a group of people that has set itself apart from a larger religious group, such as a church, often holding to beliefs that are not entirely in line with those of the larger group.

SWAT—stands for Special Weapons and Tactics; a police unit trained to deal with very dangerous situations.

telegram—a message sent in code over a wire.

tip—a small piece of information.

underground—living among people taking part in a secret, revolutionary group.

FURTHER READING

Crewe, Sabrina. *A History of the FBI*. Broomall, PA: Mason Crest Publishers, 2009.

Geary, Rick. *J. Edgar Hoover: A Graphic Biography*. New York: Hill and Wang, 2008.

Holden, Henry M. *FBI 100 Years: An Unofficial History*. Minneapolis: Zenith Press, 2008.

Kessler, Ronald. *The Bureau: The Secret History of the FBI*. New York: St. Martin's Press, 2002.

Theoharis, Athan G., editor. *The FBI: A Comprehensive Reference Guide*. New York: Checkmark Books, 2000.

Wagner, Heather Lehr. *Federal Bureau of Investigation*. Langhorne, PA: Chelsea House Publishers, 2007.

Walsh, John, with Philip Lerman. *Public Enemies: The Host of America's Most Wanted Targets the Nation's Most Notorious Criminals*. New York: Pocket Books, 2001.

INTERNET RESOURCES

http://abcnews.go.com/Blotter/FugitiveWatch/
The Blotter's Fugitive Watch is part of ABC News. This Web site includes pictures and information about fugitives on the FBI's Ten Most Wanted list, as well as fugitives on the wanted lists of other law enforcement agencies.

http://www.amw.com
The official Web site for America's Most Wanted includes details about fugitives profiled on the show, stories about how wanted fugitives have been caught, alerts about missing children, and information about host John Walsh.

http://www.fbi.gov/wanted/topten/fugitives/fugitives.htm
The official Web site for the FBI's Ten Most Wanted Fugitives list includes pictures and descriptions of the members of the list. For some fugitives, it also includes video and sound recordings.

http://www.fbi.gov/wanted/terrorists/fugitives.htm
The official Web site for the FBI's Most Wanted Terrorists list includes pictures and descriptions of fugitives wanted in connection with the attacks of September 11, 2001, the bombings of U.S. embassies overseas, the 1993 bombing of the World Trade Center, and other terrorist acts.

NOTES

Chapter 1

Page 5: "I know you're going to think . . .": Peter Duffy, "City Lore; Willie Sutton, Urbane Scoundrel," *New York Times*, February 17, 2002.
Page 7: ". . . I was walking along . . .": Steve Cocheo, "The Bank Robber, the Quote, and the Final Irony," banking.com, http://www.banking.com/ABA/profile_0397.htm.

Chapter 2

Page 17: "Don't shoot, G-men! . . . ": "A Byte Out of FBI History: 'Machine Gun' Kelly and the Legend of the G-Men," FBI online story, September 26, 2003, http://www.fbi.gov/page2/sept03/kelly092603.htm.
Page 18: ". . . I recognized the dark, heavy man . . .": Ronald Kessler, *The Bureau: The Secret History of the FBI*. New York: St. Martin's Press, 2002, p. 48.

Chapter 3

Page 21: "Give me your ten worst . . .": Kessler, The Bureau, p. 41.
Page 22: "Thomas James Holden is one . . .": Mark Sabljak and Martin S. Greenberg, *Most Wanted: A History of the FBI's Ten Most Wanted List*. New York: Bonanza Books, 1990, p. 26.
Page 23: "Alexis Flores is wanted . . .": "The FBI's Ten Most Wanted Fugitives: Alexis Flores," http://www.fbi.gov/wanted/topten/fugitives/flores_a.htm.
Page 24: "First, the individual must have . . .": "The FBI's Ten Most Wanted Fugitives: Facts on the Program," http://www.fbi.gov/wanted/topten/tenfaq.htm#1.
Page 28: ". . . a one-inch scar . . .": "The FBI's Ten Most Wanted Fugitives: Victor Manuel Gerena," http://www.fbi.gov/wanted/topten/fugitives/gerena.htm.
Page 28: "Preciado is a known member . . .": "The FBI's Ten Most Wanted Fugitives: Emigdio Preciado, Jr.," http://www.fbi.gov/wanted/topten/fugitives/preciado_e.htm.

Chapter 4

Page 32: "FBI Seeking Ex-Convict . . .": Sabljak and Greenberg, *Most Wanted*, p. 91.
Page 34: "They have a tendency . . .": Sabljak and Greenberg, *Most Wanted*, p. 179.

Chapter 5

Page 42: "In Adam's memory, I did . . .": John Walsh with Philip Lerman, *Public Enemies: The Host of America's Most Wanted Targets the Nation's Most Notorious Criminals*. New York: Pocket Books, 2001, p. 307.

Chapter 6

Page 51 "You have been exposed . . .": "The Quiet Fall of an American Terrorist," http://dir.salon.com/story/news/feature/2003/12/10/waagner.
Page 52: "On the flight . . . ": John Miller and Michael Stone with Chris Mitchell, *The Cell: Inside the 9/11 Plot, and Why the FBI and CIA Failed To Stop It*. New York: Hyperion, 2002, p. 135.
Page 55: "The men on the wall . . .": "President Unveils 'Most Wanted' Terrorists," October 10, 2001, http://www.whitehouse.gov/news/releases/2001/10/20011010-3.html.

WANTED BY THE FBI

AIDING & ABETTING. IMPORTATION, MANUFACTURE, DISTRIBUTION AND STORAGE OF EXPLOSIVE MATERIALS

RAMZI AHMED YOUSEF

Captured this day in 1995

INDEX

About the Author

Alan Wachtel has been editing and writing educational books since 2001. He maintains an air of mystery that may or may not have any basis in fact.